Recollections and Recipes
of the Winery and the Vineyards Restaurant

Recollections and Recipes

of the Winery and the Vineyards Restaurant

Patricia Pirtle and Elbert Pirtle

Copyright © 2021 by Patricia Pirtle & Elbert Pirtle.

ISBN-978-1-6379-0126-7

All rights reserved. No part of this book may be reproduced or transmitted in any form or by any means, electronic or mechanical, including photocopying, recording, or by any information storage and retrieval system, without permission in writing from the copyright owner.

The views expressed in this work are solely those of the author and do not necessarily reflect the views of the publisher, and the publisher hereby disclaims any responsibility for them.

Matchstick Literary
1-888-306-8885
orders@matchliterary.com

Table of Recipes

Pesto Sauce	22
Charles' Vineyards Dressing	31
Patricia's Salad	33
Marsala and Mushroom Sauce	34
Charles Pirtle's Herbed Braised Lamb Shanks	35
Cauliflower, Shrimp and Ginger Salad	36
Tossed Green Salad with Dill Dressing	37
Putsch's Spinach Salad	38
Festiva Corn	39
Yvonne's Shrimp Salad	40
24 Hour Slaw	41
French Onion Soup	42
Vegetable Bean Soup	44
Five Onion Soup	45
Beef Stew	47
Giant Anchovy and Garlic Crostini	48
Tiffani's Apple Wine Pork Tenderloin	49
Rueben Sandwiches	50
Pimiento Cheese Sandwiches	51
Tuna Salad Sandwiches	51
Grandchildren's Cheesy Potatoes	53
Barbecued Chicken Blackened	54
Brandied Chicken	56
Charles' Asparagus Soup	62
Chicken Marsala	63
Sweet and Spicy Chicken	64
Creamy Cabbage Casserole	65
Broccoli-Cheese Casserole	66
Aunt Mavis' Corn Casserole	67
Artichoke Quiche	68
Green Onion Cheesy Quiche	69
Paul's Fish Coating	71

New Zealand Green Lipped Mussels	72
Mother's Candied Sweet Potatoes	73
My Daddy's Favorite Recipe	78
Paige and Megan Pirtle's - Tenderloin of Pork	79
Pineapple Au Gratin	80
Pumpkin Bread	81
Cranberry-Apricot-Nut Loaf	82
Mother In-Laws Chocolate Pie	83
Charles' Apple Pie	86
"It's Pumpkin Pie for Me"	87
Pecan Pie	88
Raspberry Pie	91
Old Fashioned Chess Pie	92
Cherries in Pirtle Mellow Red	93
Aunt Mavis' Peach Cobbler	84
Brownies the Easy Way	85
Lemon Sponge Pie	96
Make Them Your Way Cookies	97
Apple Bread	99
Gingerbread	100
Rippey's Cheesecake	101
Milwaukee Cheese Cake	109
Scotch Shortbread	104
Lemon Curd	104
Scones	105
Lemon Nut Bread	106

Foreword

We wanted this to be a cookbook with a view of its beginnings, starting with the winery. The restaurant came four years later. We had the good fortune to purchase the restaurant land in 1983. The winery took most of our time. Our son Charles had worked as a chef in New York and Kansas City and had also worked for his grandmother Mary Wallace (Patricia's mother) in her (famous) drive-in restaurant in Lufkin, Texas. We suggested to him that he revive the old house with our help. Winery customers all wanted a place to have lunch. The restaurant would complement the winery and vice versa. He finally agreed, revived the old house almost single handedly and made the restaurant famous. After a while, the tail wagged the dog. This is an intimate view of the story, with recipes included.

Acknowledgements

First we want to thank our artist-illustrator friend Mary Louise Wilson for her outstanding contributions to our business. She is the person who did the art work for the cover of this book. She is the person who came up with the Pirtle logo. She did the art work for our apple wine label and the background art for the Mellow Red and Weston Bend White labels. The building in the background of these two labels is a black and white rendering of our winery building by her.

Wine labels may be changed by others. The Pirtle logo is enshrined in Indiana marble in the peak of the new building. It is guaranteed to last a thousand years.

Incidentally, the inscription in the peak of our old building is also in Indiana marble. It has been there since 1867 (not quite a thousand years yet).

Second, we appreciate the generous contributions of recollections and memories from friends who knew Charles (and us) well. You will read their stories in the book.

Third, and most important of all, we appreciate all our customers who took their time to walk up the "thirteen steps to heaven", taste the wine, and share some of their life with us. Without them, there would be no book.

~Winery History~

The land this former church stands on was purchased in the mid 1860's for one-hundred fifteen dollars. The construction of the Weston German Evangelical Lutheran Church was completed in November 1867.

The Old River Town of Weston had enjoyed growth and prosperity and had also seen it wane; for just five years after the Civil War her population had diminished from 5,000 to 1,000 residents. The organization of the new church during this period was most difficult.

During most of the latter part of the nineteenth century the congregation was besieged with financial reverses. For a number of years the Lutherans used the building for a school room. In 1888 August F Walruff purchased the church and used it for a bottling shop for his brewery. Around the turn of the century the building was sold to the more affluent African-American congregation of the Second Baptist Church of Weston.

*Winery Building
ca. 1982*

From then and into the 1930's the congregation enjoyed many social gatherings with cuisine consisting of Hickory Smoked Ham, Southern Fried Chicken, Fish dinners and Pastries. These occasions were attended by people of all faiths and races, here it is 2005 and we still hear stories of wonderful feasts and music. I have met several of the old congregation, even the piano player. Precious people, I wish I knew more.

During the 1930's many members were deceased, some had left Weston and by 1962 the congregation had dwindled to six members. The church was closed in 1963, the remaining few, transferred their membership to their church in Platte City, Missouri.

Congregation of Second Baptist Church circa 1900

In 1977 the city re-zoned the old church for business and prevented the telephone company next door from razing the building for a parking lot.

We bought the building in March of 1980. It was dilapidated but restorable.

We opened on October 1, 1980 as Weston Vineyards Winery. The building is listed in the National Register of Historic Places.

We had been operating since 1978 as Bowman Wine Cellars in the cellars of the former Royal Brewing Company est. 1842. The cellars now operate as an Irish Pub. We basically moved our cellar operation intact to our "new" location.

A significant problem was finding furnishings for wine tasting and a gift shop. Our son Charles found the perfect solution for the wine bar at Rumpel Hardware. It was a chest of drawers that Rumpel had purchased from Harry Truman's Haberdashery in the Muehlbach Hotel. He bought it when Truman went out of business. It was called a "shirt box". Rumpel was one time mayor of Weston and apparently had some political connection with Truman.

It may be possible to find pictures of the shirt box in the Truman Library in Independence, Missouri.

The Way We Were

This photo was taken in 1979 when we were operating in the old beer cellars.

At Rumpel Hardware Charles also found a new (never been used) gas heater (Heatarola) for the upstairs area, made in the 1930's. It is still operating today (2006).

Other tables, sideboards we got from a convent school and various flea markets and an antique store in Weston.

In case you don't remember, in those days, (1981-82) interest rates at the bank(s) were 21%, if you could get a loan.

We opened at the new location with Mellow Red, Apple Wine, Mead and a soft white wine. All four are still best sellers today. There is a cult following for Mellow Red.

As our label stated, Mead is honey wine. It is believed to be the most ancient of fermented beverages. It has been written that the literature of every civilization that ever existed contains references to honey wine. When we started producing Mead in 1979 there were only one or two other Mead producers in this country and I only knew one at the time. We perfected our regular Mead so that it became a best seller. We then introduced a sparkling version of our regular (still) mead. Both have won gold medals almost every year and are still best sellers.

Very Early Scene of Weston

"To our very good friend Charles Pirtle.
Mary & Charles Bradley, September 17, 1988"
This is a photo of the west side of Main Street in down town
Weston. It was taken before 1925, since there were no paved
streets before that date.
Rumpel Hardware is the second building from the right. George
Rumpel's grandfather built and lived in the house that is now
the Vineyards Restaurant. The date was 1845, for the house.

Our first press, ca. 1981

Today's press, 2001: "Just push the green button."

Ross Murray Pirtle, Age 13
In the midst of crushing 20 tons of grapes.

We still age our Apple wine in used brandy barrels. This unique wine has been popular for 27 years. In the early days of the winery business was sometimes slow in the winter. I learned to do stained glass construction, thinking that eventually I would be able to fill all the windows upstairs with stained glass.

The two front windows (with the WV) were finished in 1981 with the help of my youngest son, Ross.

I designed the window with the climbing rose motif in January 1984 and finished the upper half that year. One year later I finished the lower half.

Remember that stained glass design and construction is tedious and time consuming. Spare time became scarce as business increased. I never filled any more windows with stained glass.

Two front Windows, 1981

Stained Glass, ca. 1984

Memory

Our best memory of the Pirtles is being THE first people to sit at the new wine garden. Patricia sent one of her "boys" to get a table and history was made! We especially enjoyed seeing this after frequent trips while the work was in progress, it's nice to see hard work rewarded! Our only hope is to be the first people to break in the new place!

Jesse & Teresa Cortinas

We bought the land where the Vineyards Restaurant is located in 1983.

Restaurant Building, ca 1983

This is a watercolor painting done from a photograph taken from the winery. Anne Bollin of Weston is the artist.

Even though the building was in severe need of repair, we kept it with the thought of using it "for something" later. That story is revealed in the section about the restaurant.

Anne Bollin is the owner of the Missouri Bluffs Gallery Boutique in downtown Weston. She and her husband John have been in Weston over 20 years now. She says that the first person she met in Weston was our son Charles when she came into the winery to sell some advertising. Shortly after, she and her husband opened for business in Weston.

It is my experience in the business of wine that all the glamour is in the tasting room. Giving potential customers wine tastings and discussing their likes and dislikes was truly enjoyable for me and particularly for my wife, Patricia.

Patricia Pirtle, 1980
This was taken in the vineyard that is now our front yard. Clearly, not all the glamour was in the tasting room.

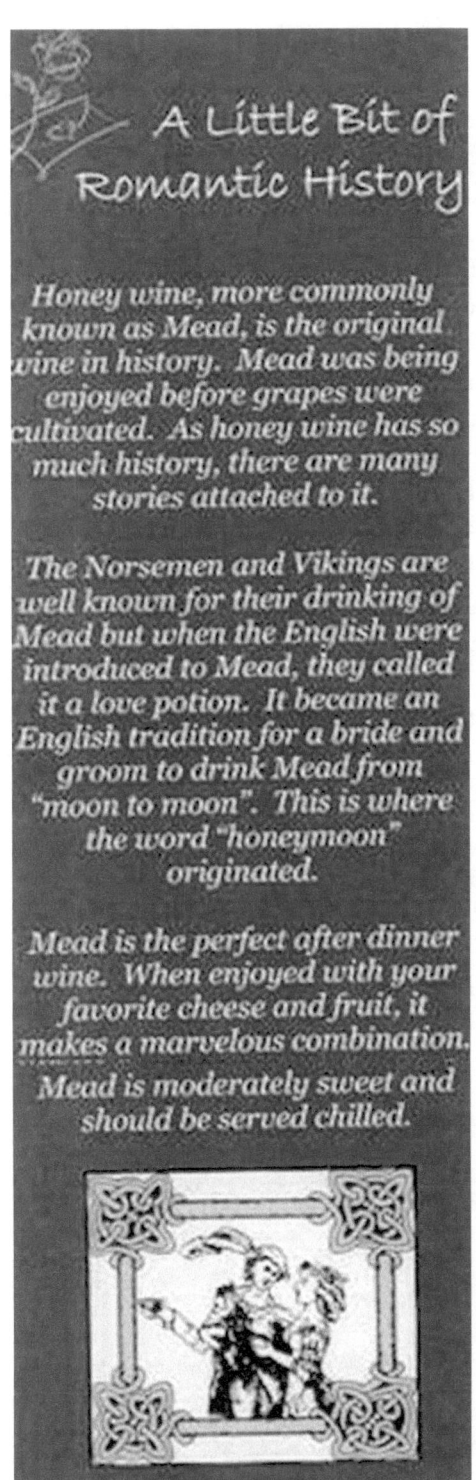

A Little Bit of Romantic History

Honey wine, more commonly known as Mead, is the original wine in history. Mead was being enjoyed before grapes were cultivated. As honey wine has so much history, there are many stories attached to it.

The Norsemen and Vikings are well known for their drinking of Mead but when the English were introduced to Mead, they called it a love potion. It became an English tradition for a bride and groom to drink Mead from "moon to moon". This is where the word "honeymoon" originated.

Mead is the perfect after dinner wine. When enjoyed with your favorite cheese and fruit, it makes a marvelous combination. Mead is moderately sweet and should be served chilled.

For years I told this little bit of history to every person who walked into the winery. One day I was at a printing co. and I said to myself, "Tell this story to the lady behind the counter and ask her to type it for you". I did and it became a bookmark.

As with the early development of most businesses, most of our days were taken up with sales, quality control, and finding new ways to attract new customers, and the usual paperwork.

Some days bring complete surprise.

Surprise, Surprise

It is a fact that the Bureau of Alcohol, Tobacco and Firearms must approve every label on every adult beverage sold in this country.

Since German immigrants built our building and the inscription imbedded on the front peak of the building was written in German, I thought that a German name or two for our wines would be appropriate.

I submitted the following names to the BATF, with the entire required ancillary wording: (1) Rosenblümchen, and (2) Goldeströpchen. They were accepted by BATF and subsequently printed and used.

My good friend Jennifer Liebnitz, who taught German and speaks it fluently, assisted me.

Rosenblümchen freely translates as "little rose flowers". We used it on various rose' wines. Goldeströpchen translates as "little drops of gold". We used it on certain soft white wines.

Most of our customers didn't read German so I had to give the above translations every time the wines were tasted. Everyone seemed to enjoy this approach. The wines were well accepted and we continued in this fashion for some years.

One day, out of the blue, we got a lawyer letter from some bunch in New York City stating: (1) They represented the German Wine Growers; (2) The name "Goldeströpchen" infringed on the name of the German wine growing area called "Goldtropchen"; (3) We must cease to use our Goldeströpchen label immediately; (4) if we didn't, they would effectively cause the sky to fall on us.

This was a shock at first. I had wanted a German name for the phrase, "little drops of gold" and had independently come up with the name.

After the adrenaline rush from the initial blow subsided, I began to consider my options, of which were only two.

I decided to continue using the Goldeströpchen label. After all, it had been approved by the BATF and it fit in with the German background of the building.

I also came to the conclusion that being sued by The German Wine Growers would be the best publicity I could get. I couldn't buy the national attention I believed a lawsuit would bring, if I shouted it to the world.

I didn't answer the letter. About a month later they called me about the label. I told them that the label was approved by BATF and maybe they should talk to BATF. They didn't fight it and I never heard from them again.

A year or so later we changed our non-varietal white wine label to "Weston Bend White".

Grapes soon to be transformed into Weston Bend White
2005

~ The Restaurant ~

The Vineyards Restaurant first opened for business October 1, 1984 by our son, Charles Pirtle. The opening was preceded by months of renovation and all the problems that always accompany such projects. The Rumpel family built the little house in 1845. They were German immigrants; some of their descendants still live in Weston. Even though I knew three families that had lived there in the 1930's thru the 60's, there were no pipes or wires of any kind in the house. The Weston fire department offered to burn it for a practice fire. Of course we declined the offer and proceeded with the renewal. Charles did most of the work himself. The restaurant building is now also in the National Register of Historic Places.

At his mother's insistence, Charles began the restaurant in delicatessen style. He served soups, sandwiches, salads and cooked omelettes on an antique 3-burner gas stove. It was an instant success. Within a year the deli equipment was out. The deli was converted to a fine dining restaurant, the first of its kind in Weston. The restaurant's 4-star status put Weston on the map. Charles' artistic taste, cooking style and vibrant personality still permeate the restaurant even though he is no longer there.

His recipes will follow along with stories of how the business progressed, memories of interesting and entertaining events that impacted the lives of his customers and us. Each and every day we hear an interesting and entertaining incident about the past and how he impacted lives. If you have some fun story to tell, please write to me. His cooking lessons were filled at all times. Some of you have stories to tell. Please write me and tell me your favorite recipe, story, etc. He moved so fast that it was hard for me to know what was happening all the time. Do you remember when I hand-wrote his menus on parchment paper?

Memory from Dorothy Donnelli

One of the most fascinating things about dining at the Vineyards was the fact that my parents lived in the home for a while when my brother was very young in the mid to late 1930's. Our family would sometimes dine in the room that had been my brother's bedroom so many years before.

The food was always excellent and we especially enjoyed the fresh ground coffee.

Dorothy Donnelli. Platte City MO

Here is one of Charles' handwritten notes on Pesto he made for one of his cooking classes. In case you can't read his handwriting, a translation follows.

Pestos

The word Pesto comes from the Italian word for paste. The most famous of Pestos most of us know with Basil and Pine nuts, Romano Cheese, Garlic and Olive Oil. Actually this is the famous pesto of Genoa, Italy. Since the word Pesto gave me free rein to do as I please here are some intriguing and exotic Pestos I have personally concocted. Use these as guidelines and with practice, get creative and concoct your own versions of a classic where anything goes.

~ Pesto Sauce ~

This is a very simple recipe. Charles Pirtle used this every day.

3 cups fresh basil leaves, firmly packed.
6 cloves garlic
1 cup freshly grated Parmesan or Romano cheese
½ cup almonds
½ cup extra virgin olive oil

In a food processor place: garlic, basil, cheese and almonds. Start the motor and pour in the olive oil in a thin stream until the mixture has the consistency of mayonnaise. Pesto will keep for several days under refrigeration.

In a sauté pan heat ½ cup whipping cream, add 2 tablespoons pesto. Heat well and serve over baked chicken breast.

I can see Charles doing just this as I type this for you. Pesto sauce is one of the first sauces I remember Charles doing. He started this in the very beginning deli phase. He actually used a mortar and pestle to grind the almonds.

The Impossible Dream before the Beginning

Plaque now mounted at corner of Restaurant

Evolution of the Restaurant Building

*The Vineyards Restaurant
In the beginning, ca. 1986*

As seen today with the front porch addition

Memory from Bernadette Youngblood

Advanced Cooking Class

Here is the story of a lovely evening at The Vineyards that brings back many wonderful memories. We were hosting a couple from Mississippi for several days as houseguests. They were good friends and we were happily making plans as to how to show them the best the Midwest had to offer. We scheduled the time that they would be with us with great care, balancing fun, shopping, golf and, of course, some "kickback" time. Obviously it would be a great choice to take them to the Vineyards for dinner one of the nights that they would be there. But wait—Let's expand on this idea.

Hmmm . . .

The cooking classes that Charles conducted had already achieved considerable renown in and around our area. We decided to set up a private class and then thought of the fun of including another couple, close friends from our 22 years in Kansas City. Each of four friends were not only gourmets, they were also gourmands. It could be a fabulous evening. Perfect idea!

Charles and I worked on the menu off and on for weeks ahead of time, adding and subtracting items for each course. This guy was a genius and it was fascinating for me to see his mind work as we tweaked the menu.

As all six arrived we were ushered into the kitchen. Charles presented each of us with a fresh cook's apron (I still have mine) and we got started. First off, he gave us a glass of one of our carefully chosen wines and then took us through the fine points of making pesto. His pesto was out of this world. There was also a newly-made batch of bruschetta and some of my favorite cheeses as well. Ever tried Danish Blue cheese topped with freshly made pesto on still-warm bruschetta? If not, you must.

Apple pie was to be the dessert so it was quickly mastered and put into the oven. Charles admitted, with some request of secrecy, that he used Pillsbury piecrusts for his pies. But his tossing the apples with just the right amount of flour, melted butter, sugar, and spices was a sight to behold.

Charles and I had chosen his fabulous Duck with my choice of cherry sauce as the main entree'. He filleted the duck breast, sautéed it quickly in olive oil and got it ready to pop into the oven. Then he prepared for cooking, but did not yet sauté, the green beans. New potatoes were scrubbed and ready to go. The salad was next—a fresh, crisp assortment of all kinds of greens. The dressing was made as we watched and took notes, but was not yet added. It was a combination of oil, several kinds of vinegars, a bit of sugar, a tad of lemon juice and various herbs.

Shrimp scampi was to be the appetizer. Keep in mind that we had been devouring cheeses, pesto, bruschetta, etc. while observing and learning from Charles. He started the garlic, butter, shrimp thing while we all watched in wonderment and then sent us upstairs right before the shrimp was ready. He also put the new potatoes on the stove and cranked up the burner.

Soon after we were seated (and had some new glasses of wine), the scampi was served and was remarkably good. The salad was next and the dressing was the perfect complement to the fresh greens.

While we were enjoying the scampi, Charles disappeared into the kitchen and finished preparing the rest of the meal.

The duck appeared, with just-rightly crisp green beans, buttered and parsleyed new potatoes, and a new wine. You can't imagine how good all of this was. Our friends enjoyed each and every bite and we were pleased to have them with us for such a pleasurable time.

The apple pie was still warm when it was served and could not have been tastier. It had just a thin overlay of ice cream with a small slice of cheddar at the side.

A bit of Brandy and some of the good coffee that Charles made topped a perfect evening.

That dinner, that evening, has to rank near the top of my list of fine, fun memories. For those of you who read this and have had the same or similar experiences at the Vineyards, I hope I have conjured some nice memories for you.

For those of you who never knew Charles or savored his productions from the kitchen, perhaps this will tell you how the Vineyards started and what a great chef Charles really was.

We, who knew him, miss him.

—Bernadette Youngblood

*Charles at work in the kitchen, with David Scott on the left
David Scott now owns and is the chef of the Avalon Cafe on Main Street,
Weston Missouri. His cooking style is very much like Charles'.*

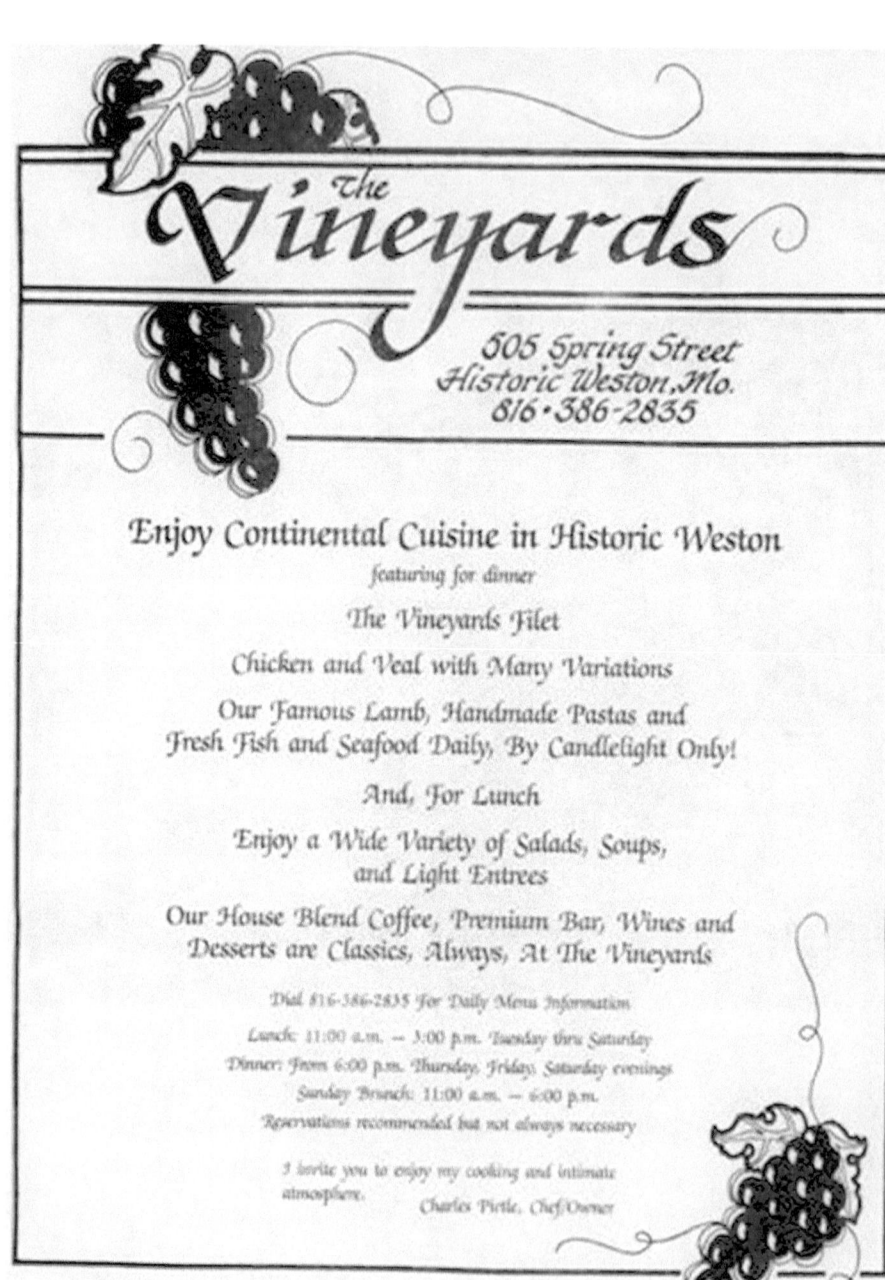

This is a general publicity brochure Charles used early on.

The actual menu had minor variations weekly. Here are some of the dishes on the dinner menu that Charles perfected and that gave the Vineyards Restaurant and Charles Pirtle their 4-star rating.

Appetizers: the appetizer list was a changing one, depending on what was fresh and in season. It might include the following:

Scampi

New Zealand green lipped mussels (recipe follows)

Baked Brie and assorted other cheeses with fresh fruit, usually grapes and strawberries and blueberries. Baked garlic (my favorite) served with this was optional.

Composed Salad crisp fresh greens topped with strips of red and green peppers and finished with his own crowd pleasing "Honey French" dressing (recipe follows). The dressing was a real winner.

Filet of Beef brushed with mild garlic flavored olive oil and charcoal grilled over grapevine cuttings; served with a rich Marsala and mushroom sauce (recipe to follow). The most common customer comment, "Probably the best filet I've ever tasted".

Grilled Salmon with fresh pesto; a marriage made in heaven.

Herb Braised Lamb Shanks So popular that reservations for them were usually made with dinner reservations (recipe follows)

Roast Duck served with a Grand Marnier sauce; rich golden exterior and juicy interior.

All the above entrees served with perfectly cooked new potatoes and fresh asparagus.

This is a copy of an actual menu handwritten for Charles by his mother Patricia.

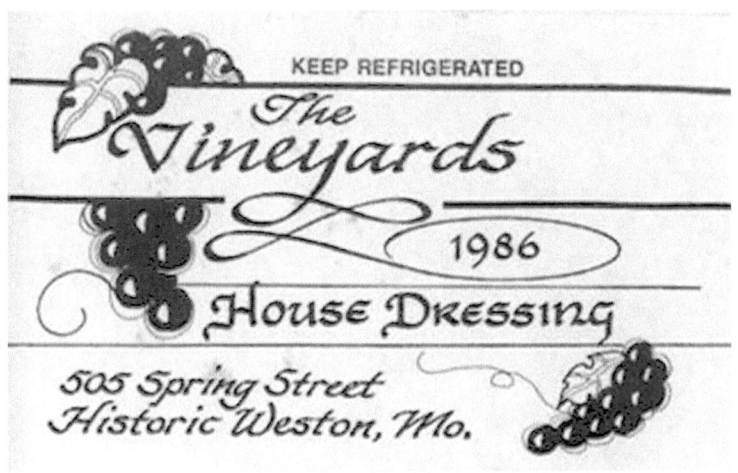

Charles' Vineyards Dressing

1 cup olive oil
½ cup honey
½ cup red wine vinegar
3 tablespoons Chili sauce
1 green onion
1 garlic clove
½ bunch fresh dill
2 tsp. Worchester sauce

Charles put everything in a food processor but the olive oil. He then added the olive oil slowly through the top.

I have had more requests for this. I have discovered that if you like more onion or other seasoning that it will remain as good, just try to suit your own palate.

Memories from Margaret T. Wilson

Charles' restaurant was such a delight. Finally a place in Weston we could take our out-of-town friends for gourmet dining. They were always greatly impressed. Westonites Mary Ann Hull, Betty Hull, Marian Gaskill, Susan Hull, Marge Hull and I met there for lunch on occasion—always asking for the 'back room' where we could have a glass of wine, a wonderful lunch and catch up on each other's comings and goings. Often Charles would bring up one of his special pies or some other dessert to tempt us and of course, we could never resist.

—Margaret T Wilson

I remember the first time I saw this beautiful woman almost 40 years ago and Charles loved and appreciated her and enjoyed each time she and her friends came to the Vineyard. They always sat in the backroom on my old, round oak kitchen table.

Patricia Pirtle

Years ago my only daughter and my first born gave me a large salad bowl on a stand. It will hold enough salad for 30 people. I thank Denise Pirtle Scarlett every time I use it and I think that she is probably the reason I am so well known for my salads. I have many memories of the children and grandchildren around this large salad bowl. It is the main attraction when we have dinner get togethers.

~ Patricia's Salad ~

I have so many ways to make a salad that I do not know where to start. Let us start with the lettuce. I usually buy three kinds of lettuce and fresh spinach. Once this is cleaned and put in zip lock bags the rest is easy. I find that getting the lettuce cleaned and dry is the most time consuming part of the preparation. Do it the day before. I use large Ziploc bags and put paper towels in with the lettuce to absorb more moisture. Now we are ready to use our imagination.

Remember a salad can be a meal or just a salad. I am going to give you ideas and the rest is up to your personal taste. Come to our annual Great Picking-up Party in September and you can enjoy this salad!

Ingredients:
Sweet Onions
Colossal Ripe Olives
Radishes
Tomatoes
Little New Potatoes (boiled and cut in quarters, salt and pepper and add olive oil) set aside.
Avocados
Celery
Italian Peppers Drained
3 or 4 kinds of cheese (yesterday I used Havarti, Blue Cheese, Sharp Cheddar and Extra Sharp Cheddar Cheese).
Pepperoni cooked and oil absorbed
Canadian bacon sliced and brown in skillet
Red pepper sliced
You get the picture. After all of your favorites are added. Coat with olive oil and toss. I never measure this because it all depends on the size of the salad. I then add red wine vinegar and toss. You can use your own dressing and there are many other foods you can add Albacore tuna in olive oil (drained), boiled eggs, and left over roast cut in pieces.
Serve with crusty French bread.

~ Marsala and Mushroom Sauce ~

2 Tablespoons butter melted in sauté pan
Add 1 cup sliced fresh mushrooms sauté until tender.
Add ½ cup Marsala
Cook until reduced
Add ½ cup heavy cream
Reduce on low heat
Serve over filet of beef, chicken breast, and pork tenderloin. Let your taste buds help you decide!

Greek Potato Salad
(Mike Lagas)

Night before scrub russet potatoes and boil slowly. Do not peel. Boil until just cooked, drain. Let sit until easily handled, peel put in refrigerator and let cool down.

Next day: Cube potatoes and put into bowl drizzle with some olive oil and vinegar. Add and alternate in layers (easier to mix). Amounts of the following ingredients. Depends on individual taste.

1. cut a red onion (amount of potatoes will determine amount of onion)
2. green onions 2-3
3. celery 2-3 spines
4. parsely-flat fresh
5. oregano
6. seasoned garlic salt
7. ground pepper

Drizzle with more olive oil and wine vinegar and toss. Salad may need additional olive oil just before serving.

~ Charles Pirtle's
Herbed Braised Lamb Shanks ~

4 lamb shanks
Salt and pepper each shank and sauté on all sides until nicely brown. Put browned shanks in large baking pan.

In a food processor add:
12 cloves garlic
2 bundles fresh dill
1 large onion
1 bunch fresh basil
1 whole green pepper

Blend ingredients and pour over lamb shanks

Then add:
2 cups Marsala Wine
1 cup Sherry
¼ cup Worchester sauce
6 fresh rosemary sprigs (whole)

Cover baking pan tightly with foil and bake at 400° for 1 hour, then at 325° for 3 hours. Serve this with crusty French bread and Pirtle Chambourcin

People rushed to get to the Vineyards for Sunday brunch hoping Charles would have leftover shanks from Saturday night and often he did, but when he didn't there were lots of sad faces so he started cooking more on Saturday night.
I hope these will taste as you remember them.
—Patricia Pirtle

~ Cauliflower, Shrimp and Ginger Salad ~

Ingredients for serving for 4 persons:

1 ¼ cups native shrimp
½ head of cauliflower
2 cups fresh spinach
1 red onion, finely chopped
3 tablespoons olive oil
1 ½ tablespoons white wine vinegar
1 tablespoon freshly grated ginger
Salt and pepper

This is how you do it:

Divide the cauliflower into small bouquets. Mix it with the shrimp, spinach, red onion, olive oil and vinegar. Season with ginger, salt and pepper.

The Bread:
1 loaf of white bread, preferably a day old
Olive oil, Salt

Cut the bread into slices and lay them on a baking dish. Drizzle the olive oil over the slices and salt to taste. Toast in the oven at 400°F until they become golden brown—about five to seven minutes.

Serve with salad.
Recipe submitted by Randy Steen

*All of Randy's recipes are well tested.

~ Tossed Green Salad with Dill Dressing ~

1/2 teaspoon Dijon style mustard
1 tablespoon white wine vinegar
1 tablespoon snipped fresh dill
¼ cup olive oil
¼ bunch of watercress—coarse stems discarded, rinsed and spun dry
2 cups loosely packed, torn, red-leaf lettuce, rinsed and spun dry.
3 cups loosely packed torn Boston lettuce, rinsed and spun dry.

In a small bowl whisk together the mustard, the vinegar, the dill and salt and pepper to taste. Add the oil in a stream, whisking and whisk until it is emulsified.

In a bowl toss together well the watercress, the red-leaf lettuce, and the Boston lettuce with the dressing and divide the salad among 4 plates.

~ Putsch's Spinach Salad ~

Before I left Rimpull in Olathe, K.S. to start our winery, in July 1978, a lovely girl that I worked with asked what she could give me as a gift and I replied "Putsch's Spinach Salad Recipe". I could not believe my eyes when she showed up the next day with the recipe. I have enjoyed raves over this. The Putsch's Cafeterias are no longer in the Kansas City area but I think of them each time I prepare this.

10oz. Package frozen chopped spinach, thawed and drained. (I like Birds' Eye)
½ teaspoon salt
1 ½ tsp. vinegar
½ tsp Tabasco
¾ cup chopped celery
¼ cup chopped onion
4 hard boiled eggs finely chopped
¾ cup diced (small) cheddar
1/3 to ½ c. mayonnaise
1/3 to ½ c. sour cream

Mix all of the above together but reserving one egg for garnish. On a lettuce leaf, put a scoop of salad, top with chopped egg and serve horseradish on the side.

This makes a very nice side dish for the holidays or at any time. Thanks to all that created this and found the recipe for me. You have given many people enjoyment and it makes for a nice story to tell as we enjoy the salad.

~ Festiva Corn ~

Sauté 1 medium onion and 3 green onions
¼ cup finely chopped green pepper
1 (2oz.) jar pimiento
Sauté in 1 stick of butter

Add: 1 (8oz.) can cream style corn
Add: 1 (8oz.) can regular corn (do not drain)
1 box Jiffy cornbread mix
1 egg beaten
1 (8oz.) sour cream
Dash of salt

Blend well. Pour into casserole and cover with buttered bread crumbs.

Bake at 350° F for 1 hour.

This was a recipe that Denise Scarlett entered in the vegetable category and was the winner in a 1990 holiday cooking contest. You will enjoy this and it is so easy.

~ Yvonne's Shrimp Salad ~

I have always requested this when I visited my sister in the Galveston, Texas area. I believe you will enjoy this as much as we did.

Coarsely chop 4 cups cabbage
Add 3 cups of large fresh boiled shrimp, de-veined and cut in half and set aside.
Add 4 boiled eggs chopped after they are cold
Pulverize in blender
Add ½ cup mayo; start off with 1/3 cup
Add ½ cup salad dressing; start with 1/3 cup
- You will know if you need more when all ingredients are added.

1 cup chopped green onion
3 garlic cloves diced fine
½ cup chopped sweet onion
1 tsp black pepper
1 cup chopped celery
¼ cup bell pepper, finely chopped

Taste as you go and season as you like, it is likely that you will need more or less mayo and salad dressing. Garnish with sliced red onion, green bell pepper and sliced hard boiled eggs.

This makes a nice summertime luncheon with hot French bread and a bottle of Pirtle Seyval, Pirtle Weston Bend White or Pirtle Apple Wine.

I hope you enjoy this. Catherine Donnelly can't go to a family reunion without this dish. I will have her notes in here soon.

~ 24 Hour Slaw ~

1 medium head cabbage, shredded
1 small onion, chopped
½ cup sugar
1 cup white vinegar
½ cup oil
1 tsp. salt
1 tsp. celery seed
1/8 tsp. pepper

Place cabbage and onion in a bowl (covered) sprinkle sugar on top, let sit. Combine remaining ingredients in a saucepan. Heat this to boiling, continue to boil for 3 minutes. Pour hot mixture over cabbage. Cover; chill for at least 12 hours before serving. This slaw will feed 8 people. It keeps well up to 10 days in refrigerator.

~ French Onion Soup ~

2 large, sweet Spanish onions
¼ cup butter
2 tablespoons flour
2 cans (10 ½ oz. each) condensed beef bouillon
2 ½ cups water
6 slices French bread, cut 1" thick
½ cup grated Parmesan Cheese
½ cup grated Swiss cheese
Peel and slice onions
Separate into rings (about 5 cups)
Sauté in butter until soft and golden, but not brown, about 20 minutes
Blend in flour

Gradually add bouillon and water stirring until smooth.

Bring to boil, reduce heat and simmer 20 minutes.

Meanwhile toast bread lightly, place slices in oven proof bowls. Ladle soup over bread. Sprinkle a little of each cheese on the top of each bowl. Baked at 425°F for 10 minutes or until cheese is melted and lightly browned.

One holiday when Paige and Megan were with me they wanted to create a soup. We did. We had potatoes, fordhood limas, onions, carrots and we boiled all this in beef broth. Catherine Scarlett, another granddaughter was one of the cooks. They loved it and we had fun together. Even the Grandfather loved it. I try to cook with my granddaughters when I am fortunate to have them around me. A couple of Christmases ago I taught Paige Pirtle to prepare Eggplant Parmesan. I can still see that accomplished smile on the beautiful young face.

Patricia Pirtle

Soup for the Cold Days

~ Vegetable Bean Soup ~

1 cup dried navy beans
2 quarts water
3 carrots diced
3 medium tomatoes, peeled and chopped
3 small onions, minced
2 stalks celery, chopped
2 cloves garlic, minced
3 tablespoons olive oil
1 tsp. salt

Wash beans thoroughly; place in a large Dutch oven. Add water; bring to a boil. Remove from heat; cover and let sit for one hour. Return water to a boil; reduce heat and simmer for 45 minutes. Add remaining ingredients; simmer, uncovered, about 30 minutes or until beans are tender. This can be changed as you add or delete the vegetables you don't want and add the ones you wish.

~ Five Onion Soup ~

This soup is not for the onion-phobic. Enjoy!

4 Tbsp. butter
2 cups finely chopped yellow onions
4 large leeks—whites only, well cleaned and thinly sliced.
½ cup chopped shallots
4-6 cloves of garlic, peeled and minced
4 cups of chicken stock
1 tsp. dried thyme
1 bay leaf
salt and pepper to taste
1 cup heavy cream
toasted croutons
grated Swiss cheese or Gruyere
snipped chives for garnish

Melt butter in pot and add yellow onions, leeks, shallots and garlic. Cook covered over low heat until tender and lightly covered, about 25 minutes. Add chicken stock, thyme and bay leaf and season to taste with salt and pepper. Bring to boil, reduce heat and cook partially covered for 20 minutes.

Pour soup through a strainer over a bowl and keep the liquid. Transfer half of onions and half of liquid to processor and process until smooth. Be sure to remove the bay leaf before processing. Mix all back together and set over medium heat. Whisk in cream and warm soup. Do not boil because it will break own the cream. Top with a few roasted croutons and chives and serve.

Memory from C.J. Dowdell

Well Done Steak—*CJ Dowdell*

Several years ago, Arch and I went to the Vineyards to have dinner. Our order was taken; Arch ordered his usual steak (well done). Charles did not like to hear that. As our lovely dinner was being served, Arch was served with a very large red tennis shoe and told this is how his steak turned out! Of course, he was finally served his well done steak by Charles. We had a wonderful evening.

*Shoe Artwork by Mary Louise Wilson

~ Beef Stew ~

2 lbs. lean boneless beef
1 onion sliced
2 cloves garlic

Brown beef in olive oil after you have floured, salted and peppered the beef. Add onion and garlic. Continue to brown.

Cover with two packages of dried onion soup mix and then cover with water. Cook in oven or on top of stove until almost tender. Add your favorite vegetables. Cook until tender. This takes almost no time on your part and it has always been a very welcome dish for my children and grandchildren. Try it and let me know. My nephew Michel Andre Font, Jr. who spent a lot of his growing up years in Buenos Aires, Argentina where the beef is considered the best . . . He loves this recipe.

~ Giant Anchovy and Garlic Crostini ~

Makes 10-12 Crostini

1 loaf of country-style bread such as Pugliese, 1 pound and at least 12 inches long.
4 olive oil packed anchovy fillets
3 cloves garlic
1 teaspoon fresh thyme leaves
¼ teaspoon balsamic vinegar
¼ cup extra-virgin olive oil
Freshly ground pepper

Preheat oven to 375° F

Cut the loaf of bread in half crosswise, then cut each half lengthwise into 1/3 inch thick slices. You should have 10 to 12 slices. Lay the slices in a single layer on rimmed baking sheets. Mince the anchovies, garlic and thyme together on a cutting board to create a paste. Scoop the paste into a small bowl, add the remaining ingredients, including 1/8 teaspoon pepper and stir to combine evenly.

Smear the mixture on the top of each bread slice, dividing it evenly. Toast in the oven until golden brown, about 12 minutes.

The crostini can be served warm or at room temperature. Leftovers can be stored in a tightly covered container at room temperature for up to 1 week. *Recipe from Randy Steen "Wild Norwegian"*

~ Tiffani's Apple Wine Pork Tenderloin ~

1 bottle Pirtle Apple Wine
1 pork tenderloin
1 apple
1 onion
1 small bag of red potatoes
1 small bag of baby carrots
3 celery stalks
4 rosemary twigs

Place the pork tenderloin into a crock pot. Pour ¾ of the apple wine over the top of the pork. Fill two wine glasses with the rest of the apple wine to enjoy while cooking. Cut the apple, onion and red potatoes (making sure the potatoes are covered with liquid) into wedges and place into crock pot. Add the baby carrots and celery on top of the potatoes. Place the fresh rosemary on last. Cook on low until pork and potatoes are tender.

~ Rueben Sandwiches ~

I am going to write and think as I go, about favorite sandwiches of my children. Scott Pirtle loved the Rueben sandwiches I made when he was at home. This sandwich is so easy and it will get you raves when you prepare it. My secret ingredient is this—Drain 2 cans of sauerkraut, add ¼ cup real mayonnaise. Put this in a saucepan. Cook and stir for about an hour or as you do other things in the kitchen. This will give the kraut a glaze and delicious taste.

1lb. Thinly sliced corned beef
1lb. baby Swiss cheese, sliced.
1 loaf pumpernickel bread, sliced
Thousand Island dressing

All the above can be doubled as the crowd gets bigger or the people are hungry. All you have to do is spread one side of the bread with Thousand Island dressing, put cheese on that side, then the corned beef and the cooked sauerkraut topped with another slice of bread. I assemble all the sandwiches and then start the grilling. In a large non-stick skillet, I add butter and olive oil. This should be hot when you put the sandwiches in the skillet. I believe in "the hotter the better". The cheese should be melted. One day I will do this easier as you can now. Use a Panini grill or any kind of grill. I started doing this over 30 years ago and continue to do them the hard way.

*Children: A good gift for Mom

~ Pimiento Cheese Sandwiches ~

Denise Pirtle Scarlett likes these as do many of my friends. It is always an easy gift to prepare and give. I have hand grated 1 ½ lbs of cheddar cheese as I talked to my sister on the phone. Might as well try to do two things at once, time is so valuable and I am not neglecting either one.

1 1/2 lb. grated cheese (your choice)
4 oz. of sliced pimiento

Enough salad dressing to bind: some like more some like less. Keep this on hand and you will always have a snack.

~ Tuna Salad Sandwiches ~

I only buy the very best tuna—solid white Albacore in oil, tastes so much better than in water but it is up to you. It will be tasty even if you prefer no oil.

¼ cup chopped sweet onion
½ chopped red apple
10 pecan halves chopped
2 tbsp. sweet relish
1 hardboiled egg very finely chopped
¼ cup mayo or salad dressing

Serve on toast or in tomato. This makes a nice sandwich or luncheon salad. Cooking and preparing food is easy, just do it with love and good ingredients!

Weston, Platte County, 1865

From the south end of Main Street looking north.

~ Grandchildren's Cheesy Potatoes ~

I had much company over the holidays and they enjoyed this dish very much, it's easy and quick.

5lbs. red potatoes, peeled and boiled (drain and put back in pot they were boiled in.)

Add salt to taste
1 stick butter
Have your hand mixer ready and mix as you add ingredients.
8 oz. Velveeta cheese (cubed), beat, add more Velveeta if you like)
8 oz. sour cream
Check for salt and white pepper

After everything is combined, put in large casserole and top with grated Cheddar cheese. Put this in the oven until bubbly.

I have never met anyone who didn't like this. I first created this for my first grandchild Jacob Ross Scarlett and he still requests it. As do Tricia, Catherine, Paige and Megan. I am working on my two youngest grandsons Maxwell and Jack. I know I will have them requesting it soon.

~ Barbecued Chicken Blackened ~
"Best Ever"

8 chicken quarters
1 cup salad oil
1 cup soy sauce
½ cup ketchup
¼ cup vinegar
1 ½ tsp. black pepper
6 crushed garlic cloves

Marinate the chicken all day in the marinade. Grill chicken for five minutes on each side to sear; then turn every 10 minutes, brushing them liberally with the marinade. Cook for about 45 to 50 minutes. By which time the soy sauce, oil and fire have produced a crunchy black crust that is delicious.

This recipe was given to me probably over 20 years ago when I had my heart set on writing a cookbook by two of the most interesting people, Michael and Carol Grimaldi. Not just interesting but handsome, beautiful and full of life. I thought if they liked this, then you surely would. Let me hear from you.

Hi there Patricia,

My name is Randy Steen and my girlfriend and I visited your winery this summer. I loved the tour and we bought several of the wines and mead. I plan on coming back again soon to get more wine. I love it!

The next time we are going to have lunch across the street at the cafe. It looks like a great place and should be listed as one of those places not to miss when you are traveling any place near Weston as well as the winery itself. I loved the arbor outside the winery. A great place to open a bottle and enjoy!

I wanted to send you a recipe that you may like to try. It calls for brandy in it, but you could use Pirtle's Port and it would taste even better. Try it and see.

Well here it is . . . and I would love for my girlfriend and I to meet you next time we are in town.

Sincerely,
Randy Steen

* Randy has contributed many recipes to this book.
—Patricia Pirtle

~ Brandied Chicken ~

This dish sounds deceptively difficult, it is not. Try it with wild rice, a green salad and French bread. Enjoy!

4 whole fryer breasts, boned and skinned
½ cup of flour
¼ tsp. salt
¼ tsp. black pepper
¼ tsp. garlic powder
¼ cup butter
½ cup apricot brandy or Pirtle Port
¾ cup chicken broth
1 tsp. basil
½ cup sour cream

Preheat a large skillet on low heat and melt the butter. Meanwhile, in a shallow dish, sift together the flour, salt, pepper, and garlic powder. Add the chicken, one piece at a time and dredge to coat.

Add the chicken to the skillet and cook for 10 minutes on each side or until chicken is browned.

Add the brandy or Port and the chicken broth. Stir and then let simmer for 10 more minutes or until the chicken is fork-tender.

Remove the chicken from the pan and place on a warmed plate. Add the sour cream to the skillet and stir to warm. Pour the warm sauce over the chicken and serve immediately. Delicious served with Pirtle Weston Bend White wine.

Makes four large servings

John Rippey

At the backdoor of the restaurant: John worked for Charles for several years. He was actually a mentor for Charles. His recipe for Beowulf's Feast follows in his own handwriting.

Beowolfs Feast

6 large appetites or 12 average

① ½ lb. thick sliced mushrooms
¼ lb. chopped scallions
¼ lb. (rings) green peppers
3 Bay leaves
Enough butter to sautee this until tender.
Once this is done, cover with a dry light wine, and refrigerate in a covered dish until called for. Remove bay leaves before adding to Kettle.

② 1 lb. can of tomatoes
½ lb. chopped carrots
½ lb. chopped celery
2 cups water
1 tsp. salt
1 cup red dry wine
Put in a pan and cook until vegetables are tender, set aside covered until needed.

③ 2 lbs. chopped beef (not ground)
1 Tbls. of coarse ground black pepper
¼ tsp. Basil
½ tsp. Thyme
1 cup water
1 lb. potatoes (in large chunks)
Arrange Beef and potatoes in pan, add water and sprinkle with spices. Cook in hot (300°) oven until potatoes are done, remove from oven and put in large kettle on stove and add all previous ingredients. Cook for 1 hr at simmer.

④ To increase to double portions see next page.

(4A) 1 lb. cooked corn (canned)
½ lb. cooked okra (canned)
1 lb. coarse cut cooked potatoes (canned)
1 cup red dry wine
3 cups Tomato Juice
1 cup canned Tomatoes
1 cup water
(this added to original recipe and simmered the last 1 hr. will double your portions)
This is a great recipe for stew and of course it gets better the longer it cooks or is reheated.

⑤ One key to the flavor of this dish is not to use any salt except what is called for in step 2 Salt or pepper to taste at the table. (do not use any salt when preparing the meat)

⑥ This is my favorite recipe for stew and I have been making this for 20 yrs.
                                                John

Inside the Restaurant

Those who have read Beowulf know that all the action took place in the "Mead Hall".

Pirtle Mead would undoubtedly be, and would have been, a great accompaniment to Beowulf's Feast.

Memory of Judy Shenefield

My memories of The Vineyards and Charles Pirtle start with the "TGIF Group". Four ladies would meet for lunch on Friday and quite often would eat at The Vineyards. The food was always excellent and it was always fun to see what dessert Charles would tempt us with from week to week. He was never too busy to give personal attention to his guests. It was not unusual for him to come in and sit with us for a chat. I will never forget the asparagus soup. It was so good. Yum, yum!

Life moves on and yet we can bring back the good memories
and enjoy them again and again.

—Judy Shenefield

~ Charles' Asparagus Soup ~

Wash and remove the tips from 1 Lb. fresh green asparagus. Simmer the tips in water until they are tender.

Cut the stalks into small pieces and place them in a saucepan.
Add 6 cups Swanson's chicken broth
1/4 cup chopped shallots or onions
1/4 cup chopped celery

Simmer these ingredients, covered, for 30 minutes. Put this into a food processor. Process until pureed.

Melt 3 tablespoons butter. Stir in, until blended, 3 tablespoons flour. Stir in slowly 1/2 cup cream.

Add the asparagus stock. Heat the soup well in a double boiler. Do not boil. Add the asparagus tips. Season the soup just before serving it with salt, paprika and white pepper.

~ Chicken Marsala ~

Here is one that will impress anyone it isn't that hard. You just need to keep an eye on your timing of the chicken and vegetables. Enjoy!

1 lb. of chicken breasts cut into chunks
1 green bell pepper sliced thin
1 red bell pepper sliced thin
1 medium onion sliced thin
2 large tomatoes diced
3 tbsp. of olive oil
½ cup of flour
1 tsp. salt
½ tsp. pepper
1 tsp. garlic powder
5 cloves of fresh garlic, chopped
6 large basil leaves chopped
1 cup Marsala dry wine
½ pound of pasta of your choice

In plastic bag place flour, garlic powder, salt and pepper, add chicken and shake well to coat. In medium sauté pan, heat 2 tablespoons of olive oil place chicken into hot pan until the chicken is golden brown. Remove chicken to a paper towel to drain off excess oil. This will take about 3 to 5 minutes. In the same pan, add the fresh garlic, bell peppers, and onions. Cook until soft—another 10 to 15 minutes. Add tomatoes, basil and wine. Reduce heat. Let simmer about 10 minutes. Add chicken and cover simmer until the liquid is absorbed and thickened slightly. Drain your pasta well. Pour into chicken mixture coat well and serve.

~ Sweet and Spicy Chicken ~

Tired of barbeque flavor? Here's an alternative that will break the monotony. Enjoy!

4 chicken breasts
1 tbsp. hot sauce
¾ cup honey
4 cups barbeque sauce (or any other kind)
3 tsp. basil leaves
1 lemon (optional)

Mix barbeque sauce, honey, and hot sauce in a large bowl.

Grill chicken.

Add lemon and basil leaves

Add chicken.

~ Creamy Cabbage Casserole ~

1 medium green cabbage, coarsely chopped
3 Tablespoons butter
¼ cup flour
1 cup whipping cream
½ cup milk
½ tsp. salt
¼ tsp. pepper
½ cup freshly grated Parmesan cheese
1/3 toasted breadcrumb
3 tablespoons melted butter

Cook cabbage covered for 10 minutes in a small amount of boiling salted water. Drain well and set aside.

Melt 3 tablespoons butter in a heavy saucepan over low heat; add flour, stirring until smooth. Cook for 1 minute, stirring constantly. Gradually add milk and whipping cream; cook over medium heat stirring constantly, until thickened and bubbly. Stir in salt and pepper.

Add cabbage to white sauce, mixing well; spoon into buttered 1 ½ quart casserole. Sprinkle with cheese, and top with breadcrumbs; drizzle with 3 tablespoons melted butter. Bake at 375°F for 25 minutes. Serves 8.

Serve this with Corned Beef and you may also add corned beef to the casserole for a complete meal. Serve with green salad and crusty French bread.

~ Broccoli-Cheese Casserole ~

2 bunches of fresh broccoli, wash and cut off stems
In a large sauce pan add broccoli. Boil in salted water until tender.

Prepare rice. (I like Uncle Ben's converted rice)
3 1/3 cup water
¼ tsp. salt
1 tablespoon butter
Bring the above to a boil

Add 1 ½ cups rice, and then stir. Reduce heat, cover and simmer for 20 minutes. Remove from heat. Let stand covered for 5 minutes or until water is absorbed. Fluff with fork.

In non-stick skillet sauté 1 med. Onion diced, 8 oz. mushrooms in 4 tablespoons butter. Set this aside. Now you have three pans of hot mixtures.

In a large mixing bowl add 12 oz. Velveeta cheese in cubes. Add broccoli. I trim more and only use the flowerettes. You can burn you hands a little bit but it is better this way and the ingredients need to be hot. Add 1 can cream of mushroom soup. Mix. Add the onions and mushrooms. (If onions and mushrooms are not in your favorite food section, leave them out.)

Last add the hot rice. After the rice is added you don't want to stir much. Blend all this and put in large casserole. Grate 1lb. of your favorite cheese over the above. Put into 350° oven for 25 minutes. This is nice if you are feeding 8 hungry people. So far everyone likes this. I get this request very often. My youngest son, Ross Murray Pirtle loves this without onions.

~ Aunt Mavis' Corn Casserole ~

<u>Serves 8</u>

2 (#2) cans of cream corn
¼ cup chopped green pepper
1 medium onion finely chopped
1 (2oz.) jar of pimiento
4 tablespoons of butter
2 tablespoons of flour
2 eggs slightly beaten
½ cup milk
½ cup bread crumbs

Sauté the green pepper, onion, pimiento in butter,
Mix corn, flour, eggs and milk in bowl and fold in sautéed vegetables. Put all in a saucepan, non stick is the best. Heat until mixture thickens. Keep stirring as it thickens.

Pour into baking dish and sprinkle with bread crumbs that have been browned in 4 tablespoons butter.

Bake in 350°F oven, uncovered, for about 30 minutes.

We were visiting Elbert Pirtle's Aunt Mavis and Uncle Ray in Olney, Texas when we were first given this dish. What a treat and what wonderful relatives. Whenever we have this dish I send a kiss upward. Aunt Mavis shared this recipe with me and now I am sharing it with you. Throughout this little book will be recipes from Aunt Mavis. By the way, we had Aunt Mavis Pirtle Perkins on this earth for 100 years.

~ Artichoke Quiche ~

1-9 inch pastry shell partially baked
2 6oz. jars of marinated artichokes
1 small onion, finely chopped
1 clove garlic, minced
4 large eggs beaten
¼ cup dry bread crumbs
¼ tsp. salt
½ lb. sharp cheddar, grated 2 cups
2 tbs. finely chopped parsley
1/8 tsp. pepper
1/8 tsp. oregano
1/8 tsp. Tabasco sauce

Drain artichokes, reserve marinade. Sauté onions and garlic in marinade for five minutes. In large bowl, beat eggs. Add bread crumbs, salt, pepper, oregano and Tabasco. Stir in cheese, parsley, artichokes and onion mixture. Pour in shell. Bake at 325° for 45 minutes.

Serves 6 people

Molly Brown's great granddaughter, Helen Benzinger McKinney, gave this to me.

~ Green Onion Cheesy Quiche ~

1 lb. bacon cooked until crisp and crumbled
¾ cup Sharp Cheddar cheese
¾ cup shredded Swiss cheese
4 Eggs, beaten
1 8oz. carton sour cream
½ cup half and half
¼ cup sliced green onions
1 tablespoon flour
¾ tsp. salt
1/8 tsp. pepper
Dash of Tabasco

Piecrust for 9-inch pie. I now buy ready-to-go piecrusts. They have been a lifesaver for me.

Prick bottoms and sides of piecrusts and bake at 400° for 4 minutes. Remove from oven and gently prick and then bake another 5 minutes. Put foil around crust before adding quiche.

Sprinkle cheeses and bacon into pastry shell. Combine the other ingredients and mix well. Bake at 375° for 45 minutes or until set. This makes a very tasty breakfast dish. Serve a fruit cup on the side. This is close to the traditional Quiche Lorraine, but with no onions. You can leave the onions out if you like. This makes a nice breakfast dish with fresh strawberries, blueberries and sliced pears.

Sometimes children won't eat the quiche but they always eat the fruit. I am always thinking about children. It is amazing how much nutrition they get from the fruit. Casey Stanton is a big fruit lover.

A note and recipe from Paul Liebnitz

Jennifer and I enjoyed many delicious lunches and dinners at the Vineyards, with Charles hovering nearby, making certain the presentation was perfect. One day toward the end of the meal that featured a stellar fish entrée, the chef paused at our table to ask:

"How was the fish?"
"Excellent", I replied, "and the asparagus was just right".
"No! I left it in 3 seconds too long!" said Charles emphatically.
"I thought it was just right", I said sincerely.
"No, I left it in too long, 3 seconds too long!"

He turned and went downstairs to the kitchen with an anguished look on his face. If only we could be as perfect as he envisioned the world.

~ Paul's Fish Coating ~

Our family fishes a lot, so we have learned to filet fish and cook bass, catfish or walleye for family fish fries. Our favorite method is still "pan-fried" with a light coating of cornmeal, flour and seasonings. Keep the mixture in a sealed container.

2/3 cup white cornmeal
1/3 cup flour
1/8 t. cayenne pepper
1/8 t. garlic powder

Coat each piece of fish with the mixture in a small amount of vegetable oil over medium heat, and preferably in a cast iron skillet.

~ New Zealand Green Lipped Mussels ~

There are so many ways to prepare this popular appetizer and it can be served as a main dish, 1lb. per person.

4 lbs. mussels
1/3 cup olive oil
1/3 cup melted butter
4 garlic cloves, peeled and finely chopped
1/3 cup finely chopped Italian parsley
Fresh ground black pepper to taste, salt to taste
4 lemons, washed, and each cut into 6 wedges

Wash the mussels in cold water and pull off their beards, if they have any. The best way to do this is to take a damp cloth and use it between your thumb and forefinger to do the pulling. This will help save your fingers and will get most of the beard out because it does not slip away. Put the olive oil into a large frying pan. Heat the oil, but not so it smokes, add the garlic and mussels and shake the pan back and forth. Stir the mussels around so they can heat evenly and all open at about the same time. The minute the mussels open, scatter on parsley, melted butter, the black pepper and salt. After a couple minutes, stir the mussels again to blend all flavors. Have heated dishes or a large platter ready, the mussels should be piping hot and served with lots of crusty French bread.

Squeeze the lemon juice on mussels before eating.

~ Mother's Candied Sweet Potatoes ~

I am going to try and recreate this wonderful dish for you. It was a tradition to always have this for Christmas and Thanksgiving.

4 medium sweet potatoes baked for 1 hour, set aside to cool.

<u>In a small mixing bowl</u>:
1/3 cup firmly packed brown sugar
2 tablespoons grated orange zest
1/3 cup white sugar
1 cup orange juice
4 tablespoons melted butter
a pinch of salt.
1 tablespoon cornstarch (Mix the cornstarch in the melted warm butter or it will not dissolve).

When the potatoes are cool enough, slice fairly thin and arrange in 1 ½ quart casserole that has been buttered. Add mixture on top of potatoes and bake at 350° for 60 minutes.

My mother, Mary Lee Murray Font Wallace always decorated them with orange and lemon slices, they were the best. All her grandchildren loved them. This is something for Thanksgiving, Christmas or Easter. Cook the sweet potatoes the day before and put in refrigerator, this will save you time. It looks and smells like Mother's but something is missing, Mother isn't here. Give your mother a hug and start your own traditions so you children and grandchildren will feel like they do about my mother. My granddaughters Paige and Megan Pirtle always ask me if this is our tradition when I am doing something. I love it!

Here is a photo of Charles and his dad taken on an early spring day in the mid 1980s.

His grandfather on his mother's side of the family was Charles Michel Font, a famous chef. He only saw his grandson a few times. The following shows striking similarities in talent and personality.

"A Chef Who Looked Like a Movie Star and Prepared Food Fit for a King Who Became the Toast of Texas"

Marge Crumbaker—Houston Post Society Editor

Right on the curve, when multi millionaire Texans were beginning to define themselves, a French chef arrived in Houston. He was Charles Michel Font. Charles dazzled the richest of the rich. Not only was he handsome as in Errol Flynn and Clarke Gable—but Charles worked his magic in the kitchen at a time when there was not a lot of magic going on in Houston, the home of big rich. No matter how much money you had or how sophisticated you became, your places for fine dining were limited. Finally, the wild-catters, real estate entrepreneurs, and shipping magnates formed their own private clubs with names like The Petroleum Club, The Ramada Club, and The Houston Club and if you didn't have a zillion or two, you couldn't eat there—Member's only and beautiful grub. Charles introduced the wealthy to things like Pompano baked in a paper bag and exotic tropical fruit salads topped with delicate dollops of ice cream so green it just blew the minds of all those newly minted genteel tycoons. The highpoint of an evening for the wealthy was to receive a visit in the dining room from Charles who always took time to change into crisp white chef's attire. Charles was a rock star for certain. Early into his life in Houston he met a beautiful Texas girl named, Mary Lee Murray. She took one look at him and whispered to a friend, "He's mine even if I never get him." The worldly Charles and Mary Lee soon married. In true French fashion, Charles named their children. There was Patricia, Rosette, Yvonne, Michel, Charlotte and Paulette.

Charles Michel Font, maternal grandfather of Charles Pirtle

New Oak Wine Barrels for '05 Vintage

~ My Daddy's Favorite Recipe ~
Beef Stroganoff

2 tbsp. oil
1 ¼ (2lbs.) cubed beef
½ garlic powder
1 tbsp. worcheshire
2 cups sliced fresh mushrooms
2 cans cream of mushroom soup
1 (16oz.) sour cream
Salt and pepper
Cooked wild rice for serving

Season beef generously with salt and pepper and cut into ¼'s.

Heat 2 tablespoons oil in a large skillet over high heat, add meat to pan and brown for about 1 minute on each side.

Add worcheshire and garlic powder and let simmer for 5 minutes. Add mushrooms and cook them until just tender, about 6 to 8 minutes. Set aside.

In a large pot or Dutch oven, mix together thoroughly the sour cream and cream of mushroom soup. Add meat/mushroom mixture and stir until meat is coated. Cover pot and bake at 350°F for 2 hours.

Serve over wild rice or egg noodles.

Recipe by Barbara Pirtle, wife of Ross Pirtle
Acknowledged by Paige and Megan Pirtle

~ Paige and Megan Pirtle's
~ Tenderloin of Pork ~

1 cup bourbon
1 cup low sodium soy sauce
4 Tablespoons brown sugar
Black pepper

Mix all of the above; pour over 2 small Pork tenderloins; poke hole in meat; marinate overnight; turn over once or twice.

Preheat oven to 325° F. I use a glass casserole to marinate and to cook the meat. Bake for 1 hour, 30 minutes.

My granddaughters like rice with this and the sauce is very good with the rice. There are also times that I sauté mushrooms with rice.

This satisfies the young and the old. Serve with salad and crusty French bread.

~ Pineapple Au Gratin ~

1 (20oz.) can pineapple tidbits (do not drain)
¾ cups sugar
1/3 cup flour

Mix all of the above and pour into buttered casserole dish. Top with 1 cup shredded cheese, then top with 1 roll of crushed Ritz crackers. Bake at 350° until hot and bubbly.

Let sit for a few minutes before serving.

This is a nice side dish with pork, ham or anything you wish.

Recipe submitted by Shirley Godfrey

~ Pumpkin Bread ~

1 can of pumpkin
1 cup pecans or walnuts (chopped)
1 cup of vegetable oil
3 cups sugar
½ tsp. salt
4 eggs
1 tsp. nutmeg
1 tsp. cinnamon
2/3 cup water
3 and 1/3 cups flour
2 tsp. soda

Use a hand mixer and blend everything together. It makes no difference how you add the ingredients. Use shortening and flour to coat a large bundt pan. Bake for 1 hour at 350° F.

This can make a great holiday bread to give as gifts. You can use smaller pans.

~ Cranberry-Apricot-Nut Loaf ~

My husband's stepfather Joe A. Dickie, whom we had in our lives for over 40 years, loved this bread. He loved apricots and Elbert's mother Emma Jane Scott Pirtle Dickie, was a real chocolate lover. For birthdays and holidays we would order their goodies from Andres'. On many occasions I would cook their favorites.

1 cups all purpose flour
¾ cup sugar
1 tablespoon baking powder
½ tsp. salt
1 cup diced dried apricots
1 cup chopped cranberries
½ cup coarsely chopped walnuts or pecans
2 eggs
¼ cup milk
¼ cup melted butter
1 tsp. grated lemon zest

Combine flour, sugar, baking powder, and salt in large bowl. Stir in apricots, cranberries, and nuts, coating well. Make a well in the center of the mixture.

Beat eggs slightly in small bowl; stir in milk, butter and lemon zest. Pour in center of flour mixture; stir until dry ingredients are moistened. Pour batter into a greased and floured loaf pan. Bake at 350° for 1 hour or until loaf tests done. Let cool in pan for 10 minutes. Remove to wire rack and cool completely. I made him an apricot nut loaf and many others and won him over totally. Like I said, "nothing says I love you like something you cook yourself".

~ Mother In-Laws Chocolate Pie ~

Now for my mother-in-law who was harder to win over but I believe I did. This chocolate pie will win you many compliments.

1 ¼ cups sugar
½ cup cocoa
1/3 cup cornstarch
¼ tsp. salt
3 cups milk
3 egg yolks
3 tablespoons melted butter
1 ½ tsp. vanilla extract
1 baked 9 inch pie shell

Combine sugar, cocoa, cornstarch, and salt in a heavy non-stick saucepan. Mix well to remove lumps. Gradually add in milk, stirring until blended. Cook over medium heat, stirring constantly. Remove from heat; stir in butter and vanilla. Immediately pour into baked pastry shell. The meringue is very easy: Beat 3 egg whites with ½ teaspoon vanilla with electric mixer until foamy. Add 6 tablespoons sugar, 1 at a time. Beat 2 to 3 minutes or until stiff peaks form and sugar dissolves. It is important to seal edges of the pie with the meringue. Bake until golden brown. This will bring you many raves and happy faces. The egg yolks should be beaten and blended into a small amt. of chocolate mixture before being added.

"Mom . . . You just ate the Polish General's Apple Pie!"

September 18, 1994, 6 p.m.

I was preparing to close the winery when Charles ran up the stairs.

"Mom, I have no help and I have 33 hungry people coming for dinner in an hour!"
"Okay Charles, I'll be there to help."

Charles prepared the food, while I arranged all flowers, candles and set the tables. He hadn't told me who was coming to dinner. All 33 were military officers.

Lieutenant Colonel through General, from the Eastern Bloc: Poland, the Czech Republic, Bulgaria and Germany. They were also accompanied by some Ft. Leavenworth officers; 33 big men who literally filled the whole restaurant. And each spoke with a different accent.

They munched their way through large quantities of appetizers: Green Lipped Mussels, Brie with fruit and garlic, shrimp scampi. And then they feasted on Lamb Shanks, Filet of beef and Sea Bass. Charles went from table to table serving copious amounts of wine and brandy, while I did the cleanup work.

The apple pies were in the oven. Only the two of us, Charles and I, were taking care of the group. I was so hungry. Earlier I had managed only to grab a piece of bread and some garlic.

After the pies were served there was a lonely piece remaining in the bar area. I sliced off a small piece to check it out and Charles caught me:

"Mom, you just ate the Polish general's apple pie!"

I told him to reheat the pie and put some extra ice cream on it. It must have worked. We still have the guest book they all signed.

"This is the most delightful place that I have found during my stay in the U.S.A."
—General Kovatchev Bulgaria

At the end of the meal, each man took out his wallet with currency of his native country, signed it, and gave it to Charles.

Notice the above picture, one Christmas I took this photo before we ate our main course. These are the three main pies.

~ Charles' Apple Pie ~

Every time I ask Paige Pirtle what her favorite pie is she says, "Uncle Charles' Apple Pie". I am not sure how old she was when she first tasted it but my guess is she was probably around 3 years old. Here it is Paige:

5 Jonathan apples cored, peeled and sliced thinly. In small bowl mix ¼ cup flour, ¾ cup sugar and ½ tsp. cinnamon. Also add ¼ cup lemon juice, ¼ cup melted butter. Add apples and blend.

Bake at 400° F for 10 minutes and then set at 350° for 45 minutes or until golden. Cover crust with foil the entire baking time. Eric Wells, an expert on Apple Pie gave this a five star rating.

~ "It's Pumpkin Pie for Me" ~

1 can Libby's canned pumpkin (The recipe on the can is excellent). Here is another version, which I like:
1 15 oz can pumpkin
1 can eagle brand condensed milk
2 jumbo eggs beaten
2 tsp. pumpkin pie spice
1 tsp. cinnamon

Mix all of this together and bake at 425° for 15 minutes and then at 350° for 35 minutes. Cover edges of crust with foil during cooking. I hope you like this pie.

My granddaughter had many songs that she sang to me. One was a Halloween pumpkin pie song so whenever I make our pumpkin pie, I smile and remember my Megan Elizabeth Pirtle singing to me.

Grandfather Pirtle remembers the words as he heard them sing it many times . . .

Three little pumpkins in a pumpkin patch, watching the moon and the witches fly past. The first little pumpkin said "my skin is much too green but I'll be orange by Halloween,"
The second little pumpkin said, "it's a jack o-lantern I will be"' the third little pumpkin said "it's pumpkin pie for me." Then they all sang out. WHOOO . . ."

These are some very precious memories.

~ Pecan Pie ~

4 Eggs
¼ tsp. salt
¼ cup melted butter
1 ¼ cup white karo syrup
1 ¼ cup sugar
1 tsp. vanilla extract
1 cup chopped pecans
1 unbaked pie crust

Beat eggs with a wire whisk. Add salt, butter, syrup, sugar and vanilla; mix well.

Pour into unbaked pie shell. Sprinkle with pecans. Bake at 350° F for 50 minutes. Cover rim of crust with foil for the entire cooking time.

My granddaughter Tricia loves this pie. I have gotten out of many jams with this pie.

Memories—Jennifer Liebnitz

One of my first memories of Charles Pirtle was a persistent little bundle of energy that was running headlong for the swimming pool on a very warm day. I was certain—as I think his mother was—that the 9 year old intended to jump into the pool, clothes and all. When Charles saw what he wanted, he went for it. Even as an adult, he pursued things with an intensity that set him apart from others.

Later Charles frequently asked me to play the harp at the Vineyards. On those evenings he listened from the kitchen below. He made specific requests, "Canon in D", "Fly Me to the Moon", "Stairway to Heaven", etc. which he would ask me to repeat if anything interrupted his concentration on the music. I can easily imagine him at the top of the stairway, looking at us, checking our presentation and enjoying beautiful music . . .

Jennifer Liebnitz with Love

Memory—Mark Shenefield

    I worked for Charles for a summer when I was 16 and what I remember most was his way about the kitchen, he was everywhere. Doing this and that with the zest of an artist, working his craft in the heat of the moment. Taking the simplest items and bringing out the best in each one with the skill of a master-craftsman shaping a fine piece of rosewood.
    For Charles, preparing dishes was like singing, and boy could he carry a tune! I will always remember the little black hibachi setting on top of the stove and the savory meat he'd cook in it, the wooden rack that hung on the door that I'd made to hold his utensils, the chocolate mint cheesecake and vanilla bean ice cream he'd serve, the way he taught me to cook asparagus and how wonderful his asparagus soup was, how to properly shake water from the head of Romaine lettuce and the day he threw a hot pan right by my head and into a tub full of soapy water. He was a bit feisty sometimes too.

—Mark Shenefield

~ Raspberry Pie ~

Charles had a way with pies. He always took them out of the oven and walked through the restaurant. The aromas filled the rooms and there seldom was any leftover pie. Here is one of Charles Pirtle's signature pies as remembered by Jennifer Liebnitz, my lifelong friend.

Pie crusts for 9 inch pie

½ cup brown sugar
2 bags frozen berries or use fresh when available
1/3 cup Chambord (Raspberry Liquor)
4 tablespoons cornstarch

It is just that simple. In a bowl mix the 4 ingredients. Pour into pie crust and use a lattice top or whatever you desire. Bake at 400°F for 30 minutes. It should be bubbly and golden. You may use blackberries or a combination of the two.

~ Old Fashioned Chess Pie ~

In mixing bowl:
Beat 4 large eggs
Add ¼ cup half and half
Add ¼ cup melted butter

In another mixing bowl mix:
2 cups sugar with 1 heaping tablespoon of flour and 1 heaping tablespoon yellow corn meal.

Gradually add dry mixture to egg mixture. Pour into a 9 inch pie shell (unbaked). I use *Pillsbury Just Unroll Pie Crusts*. It sure cuts your work in half and they are excellent. I remember the days the kitchen and I were covered in flour. Bake at 325° for 55 minutes or very close to an hour. Bake it all the way with foil around the crust. If you like you can bake Lemon Chess Pie, just do not use half and half and add ¼ cup freshly squeezed lemon juice and the zest of one lemon.

~ Cherries in Pirtle Mellow Red ~

1 lb. dark sweet cherries, pitted
1 cup Pirtle Mellow Red
¼ cup sugar
½ tsp. ground cinnamon
2 tsp. cornstarch
¼ cup red currant jelly

Combine cherries, wine, sugar and cinnamon in a medium saucepan. Bring to a boil.

In a small bowl, combine cornstarch and red currant jelly. Stir in hot cherry mixture. Simmer 1 minute, stirring constantly. Cover, cool 5 minutes.

Serve warm or cold with your favorite vanilla ice cream. It makes for an impressive dessert and is very simple. I like it warm; sipping Mellow Red makes it even a more impressive dessert.

~ Aunt Mavis' Peach Cobbler ~

1 stick butter
¾ cup sugar
¾ cup all purpose flour
2 tsp. baking powder
Dash of salt
¾ cup half and half
2 cups sliced peaches (I use 2 cans Freestone slices in heavy syrup)

Melt butter in a 2 quart baking dish. Combine ¾ cup sugar, flour, baking powder and salt. Add half and half, stir until mixed. Pour batter over butter in baking dish. <u>Do not stir</u>. It is important that you do not stir. Add the peaches, juice and all. Mix ¼ cup sugar and 1 tablespoon cinnamon together. Sprinkle over peaches etc. Bake at 350 ° for one hour.

This recipe came from Elbert's Aunt Mavis Pirtle Perkins. We had her on this earth for 100 years. Each time I cook this cobbler I send a kiss upward and you will also, I promise.

If you don't have half and half, you can use milk and if you don't want the cobbler to taste as sweet, use peaches in light syrup.

~ Brownies the Easy Way ~

First of all I believe in cutting corners when it does not compromise the taste.

Buy Betty Crocker Original Supreme Brownie Mix with syrup pouch. Follow directions on the back of the box. I use 2 eggs.

The icing is the crowning finale:
Cut 6 oz. pecans finely
1 stick softened butter
1 tsp. vanilla
Powdered sugar
Half and half

Blend the butter with the powdered sugar, a little at a time. Add more sugar to thicken and half and half to thin. Add pecans and vanilla. It should be nice and thick.

After brownies are done, immediately spread icing over hot brownies. Gently spread over top. This will make the icing glaze and taste like candy. I call this "Brownies with Butter Nut Icing".

If you don't like pecans or prefer chocolate, just substitute with 2 tablespoons cocoa.

Once you start making icing like this and see how easy it is, you are sure to continue to experiment.

~ Lemon Sponge Pie ~

<u>Pie Crust</u>: Sift into mixing bowl: 2 cups pastry flour or 1 ¾ cups all purpose flour, 1 teaspoon salt Add 2/3 cup vegetable shortening Mix or cut in with pastry blender until the mixture is in even bits, about the size of peas.

<u>Put in a cup</u>: 1/3 cup ice water Sprinkle it over the flour by tablespoonfuls, stirring it in with a fork until just enough has been added so that you can pat the dough lightly into a ball. Handle the dough as little as possible and do not knead it.

Wrap the dough in wax paper or foil and chill it. (Enough for a 9 inch two crust pie and some tarts). I bake the leftover pieces with a little sugar and cinnamon or use Betty Crocker Pie Crust Cubes.

<u>Cream together</u>:
1 cup sugar
2 tbs. flour
2 tbs. butter
2 yellows of 2 eggs
1 cup milk
1 speck of salt

Mix thoroughly. Grate rind of 1 large or 2 small lemons. Add juice from lemon and rind to mix above. Whip whites of 2 eggs, add speck of baking powder. Beat until nicely frothy but not stiff. Then fold into mixture. Pour into unbaked crust which as been chilled. Bake in preheated oven, 450° for the first 10 minutes, and then reduce to 350° until pie is firm, about 25-30 minutes. I sometimes put a loose foil cover over it to keep the top from getting too brown. Cool 10 minutes. Best when warm, enjoy!

Recipe of Addie Lou Pirtle, from Klaire Pirtle

~ Make Them Your Way Cookies ~

2 cups all purpose flour
1 tsp. baking powder
¾ tsp salt
1 ½ stick butter (room temperature)
1 cup sugar
1 egg (I use Jumbo)
¼ cup milk
1 tsp. vanilla

There are so many different variations but the above will get you started on some of the best cookies you have ever tasted.

Sift flour with baking powder and salt. Cream butter in mixing bowl, gradually add sugar; continue creaming until light and fluffy. Add egg, milk and vanilla, beat well. Blend in sifted dry ingredients gradually. Drop by rounded teaspoons full onto non greased cookie sheet. Bake at 375° for 15 minutes, until golden brown. Now for the fun!

Instead of milk, add ¼ cup orange juice and ½ cup chopped pecans or walnuts. If you wish use lemon juice but only 1/8 cup and 1/8 cup milk. I also use Apricot nectar. There are so many variations that work, you can let your creative mind go and have fun, as long as you substitute the ¼ cup milk for the liquid of your choice. I do hope you enjoy these as much as my grandchildren and I have. A lovely lady introduced me to this idea. Her name is Lucile L. Jones. Thank you Lucy, Create and Enjoy!

A typical day in the tasting room at the winery.

Rose Bollin (far left), Denise Scarlett (center)

~ Apple Bread ~

1 cup sugar
½ cup shortening
2 eggs
1 teaspoon vanilla
2 cups all purpose flour
1 teaspoon baking powder
1 teaspoon baking soda
1 teaspoon ground cinnamon (if desired)
½ teaspoon salt
2 cups chopped pared apples (about 4 medium)
½ cup chopped nuts
½ cup raisins
1 tablespoon sugar
¼ teaspoon ground cinnamon

Heat oven to 350°F. Grease bottom only of loaf pan, 9 x 5 x 3 inches. Mix 1 cup sugar, the shortening, eggs and vanilla. Stir in flour, baking powder, baking soda, 1 teaspoon cinnamon and salt until smooth (batter will be thick). Stir in apples, nuts and raisins. Spread in pan. Mix 1 tablespoon sugar and ¼ teaspoon cinnamon; sprinkle over batter. Bake until wooden pick inserted about 1 inch from center comes out clean, 50 to 55 minutes. Immediately loosen sides of loaf from pan; remove from pan. Cool completely before slicing.

Makes 1 loaf.

~ Gingerbread ~

Cream together:

½ cup sugar
¾ cup Crisco

Add: 3 whole eggs, beat well

Add: 1 cup dark molasses to which has been added 1 heaping tsp. soda

Sift together:
3 cups flour
1 tsp. ginger

Add the flour mixture alternatively with 1 cup buttermilk. Bake in rectangle pan that has been well greased in 350° oven for about 30 minutes or longer.

*Recipe received from Mrs. Grosenbacher,
Houston, Texas—1937*

~ Rippey's Cheesecake ~

16 squares of graham crackers
3 tsp. sugar
2 tbs. melted oleo or butter

Grind or use rolling pin. Mix sugar and oleo in with fork

Filling:

9 or 10 oz. of cream cheese
1 cup sour cream
2 eggs
½ cup sugar
½ tsp. vanilla
½ tsp. almond
½ tsp. lemon extract or fresh

Bake at 375° for 20 minutes.

Topping:

1 cup sour cream
1 tsp. sugar
A few drops of vanilla, almond or lemon

Bake at 475° for 5 minutes.

Refrigerate at least 6 hours before serving. Garnish with cherries or strawberries, etc.

Memories from Jeanette Land

I have so many precious memories, probably because we have been such close friends of the Pirtles for so many years. Let us start with my first memory of celebrating Ross Pirtle's high school graduation on the front porch of The Vineyards. This was May 1986. What fun and what food! We have eaten in the back room of the Vineyards and in the wine garden with relatives from Canada, England and all over the U.S. This was always where they wanted to go to buy wine and enjoy food and wonderful conversation.

Another memory comes to mind; this was the occasion of Patricia and Elbert's 40th Wedding Anniversary, February 21, 1997. Charles, their oldest son and Denise, their beautiful, only daughter asked if I would like to help. With one stipulation—I had to keep it to myself, as this was a surprise for their parents. Scott, Ross and all the grandchildren were going to be there. I dug out my finest linens (used only for special occasions). I ordered my anniversary cake. The cake was decorated with Patricia's maiden name and Elbert's name and a huge yellow rose (fitting since they both came from Texas). I also made my famous cheesecake. The recipe will follow. When my husband and I walked into the winery, all we could do was gasp! The tables were laden with foods you would expect to find at the very finest restaurants. Charles and Denise beautifully arranged them. The light softly flickered from the many candles, which were highlighted by their brass candleholders. Bouquets of fresh flowers everywhere and the strains of soft music coming from the harpist, everything was perfect. What a festive occasions this was, especially when Patricia and Elbert walked through the door. We have pictures of both of them . . . completely stunned. This family is a very special family and means so much to my family.

Jeanette Land is a life long friend and one of the best cooks I have ever known and I have known a lot. Her recipes are totally authentic. Try them and you will know what I mean.

—Patricia Pirtle

~ Milwaukee Cheese Cake ~

1 lb. marshmallows
¾ cup milk
2 8oz. containers of cream cheese
2 cups (1 pint) whipping cream

Place marshmallows and milk in double boiler and stir until all marshmallows are melted. Pour into LARGE bowl and set aside to cool slightly.

Whip cream until stiff peaks. Gradually fold into mixture. When completely incorporated pour on to graham cracker crust in spring form pan. This will come to the top of the pan. Refrigerate for 4 hours.

~ Scotch Shortbread ~

1 lb. butter (NO SUBSTITUTE)
1 cup powdered sugar
3 cups sifted flour
¾ cup corn starch (or 1 cup rice flour)

Blend butter and sugar. Add flour and corn starch. Mix well until all ingredients are completely blended.

Spread onto buttered cookie sheet, prick all over with fork and bake at 325° for 45 minutes to an hour. Cut into bars while still warm but leave in pan until cool.

PLEASE NOTE: These cookies are a very pale color. If you prefer you can leave them in the oven a little longer to brown.

~ Lemon Curd ~

Juice of 4 lemons
4oz. butter
5 eggs
1lb. sugar (2 cups)

Beat eggs, combine with sugar, lemon (zest of lemons) and butter in double boiler. Stir until sugar is dissolved. Cook over boiling water stirring often until mixture thickens. This does not take long. Pour into jars. I leave my jars on the counter until cooled. Then place in fridge.

This is the simplest recipe and works every time. This makes a very nice sauce for pound cake. My Jeanette Land cooks this for me all the time.

Patricia Pirtle

~ Scones ~

2 cups all purpose sifted flour
2 tsp. baking powder
½ tsp. salt
3 tablespoons sugar
1/3 cup butter
1 egg
½ cup buttermilk (milk or cream)
½ cup currants (or raisins)

Using a mixer blend all dry ingredients into butter; add currants. Mix buttermilk and egg together and pour over dry ingredients. Mix lightly with fork. Roll out ½ inch on floured board. Cut with 2 inch cookie cutter and place on buttered baking sheet. Brush tops with egg white or milk and bake in preheated oven 400° oven for 15-20 minutes or until VERY lightly browned. Remove to cooking rack.

This recipe makes about 10 scones

Recipe from Jeanette Land, England

~ Lemon Nut Bread ~

¾ cup butter
1 ½ cup sugar
3 eggs
2 ½ cups all purpose flour
¼ tsp. salt
¼ tsp. soda
¼ cup buttermilk
zest of 1 lemon
¾ cup chopped pecans
juice of 2 lemons
¾ cup powdered sugar

Combine room temperature butter and sugar, creaming until light and fluffy; add eggs, beating well. Combine dry ingredients add to creamed mixture, beginning and ending with buttermilk; stir just until all ingredients are moistened. Stir in lemon zest and pecans.

Spoon this into a greased and floured loaf pan. Bake at 325° for 1 hour and 15 minutes or until bread tests done, cool 15 minutes and remove from pan.

Combine lemon juice and powdered sugar; stir well. Punch holes in top of warm bread with a toothpick; pour on glaze. Cool.

This is a treat with coffee for breakfast or afternoon tea.

This started off as a cookbook but we decided to bring in the Vineyards and Winery and lots of history. I would love to hear some of your stories.

Patricia Pirtle
PO Box 247
Weston MO 64098

Let me know if I can use your name or not.

This is a letter from a lady who helped put Weston on the map and was also an inspiration to many people who were in business in Weston. She saw the importance of beauty and history and worked hard at ways that others could not and was not afraid to say so.

Little did I know that she was Charles Pirtle's first Weston customer, when I asked her to write a memorable time at the restaurant? What follows are some of her first memories.

Memory—Marian Gaskill

I guess my first memories of Charles and the Restaurant date back to its opening. We, John and I, had been watching the restoration of the house on Spring Street and were pleased when we learned it would be a restaurant. Back in 1948 when John and I married, and I moved to Weston from Kansas City, Lee's Sandwich Shop on Main Street was the only eatery in town. Great for hamburgers, but if we were having guests for dinner; it was up to me to do the cooking. So the idea of a good restaurant was really appealing. Thus, we watched for the date of the opening of the Vineyards, and along with son Jeff, stopped there for dinner on its first day in business. Charles was pleased to see us, and we were served, by him, an excellent meal. I don't remember the menu; just that it was really special food. Charles presented us with the bill, and said, since we were his first Weston customers, he was asking half the regular price! We returned many times, often with guests, for the amazing food which Charles created. Our special occasions were often celebrated at the Vineyards, including our 40th wedding anniversary, in May 1988, when Charles closed the restaurant in order to serve our group there. We Miss Him!

Marian W. Gaskill

Jerry Ann Beadles' Memories of Charles

My friendship with the Pirtle family began in the mid-nineteen eighties. I first met Charles, when he was remodeling the Rumpel House for his new restaurant, The Vineyards. While running the winery, I watched him concentrate, paint, hammer and saw, on his renovation of this town landmark. The Pirtles saved the building from demolition and turned it into a "new" landmark for the town of Weston. Charles' idea for keeping the Antebellum originality of the house elicited raves from all who dined by candlelight amid antique furnishings and décor. But more than the ambiance was Charles' rare talent as a chef. He could take the simplest of items and turn them into a gourmet delight. His sauces were the stuff of culinary dreams. I remember his antique stove that he first opened his kitchen with. He was so proud to have found that treasure. He then added dining to the exterior of the restaurant, the front porch, with a view of the quiet street and the winery, and the back terrace with a view of his own vegetable and herb gardens. The small intimate interior dining rooms were also an attraction for those seeking a dining experience with Victorian flavor.

—*Jerry Ann Beadles*

Jerry Ann Beadles reminded me of Charles' garden of vegetables and herbs and how people dined on the back terrace with a good view of his garden as they enjoyed the fresh vegetables and herbs he grew for them. The photo (above) tells it all.

Picking crew in front of I-29 Highway sign at our vineyard.

Memories—Cynthia Hicks

My first memory of the Pirtle family was in 1969 in Westwood, Kansas, when I received a warm welcome from them as a 'new' music teacher at Westwood View Elementary School. Even then, as now, Patricia's smile gave encouragement and inspiration. Through the years I feel that I've known the Pirtle family through wonderful stories and achievements that have been shared with me.

As the years went on, I was always pleased to hear about the Pirtle family, the winery, and news about the children. You can imagine how special it was when I heard about The Vineyards Restaurant. One time when I visited the restaurant Charles came upstairs and there was classical recorder music in the background. With a twinkle in his eye, he asked if I liked the music, and of course, I smiled and complimented his choice. I cannot tell you how many times I have enjoyed dining at The Vineyards—and almost always with a visit from Charles.

Two more memories about The Vineyards: My mother was visiting several years ago and mentioned to Charles how delicious the apple pie was. He replied that this was really a compliment as he knew she was a great cook. What charm! And my husband, Ed and I have celebrated several anniversaries at The Vineyards. So Ed and I send our congratulations and very best wishes to each member of the Pirtle family for the years of success with the Pirtle Winery and The Vineyards restaurant. Just know that you mean a lot to our family, and we look forward to more wonderful memories!

Memories—Judy Turner Davis

I started at The Vineyards when Charles was just beginning to switch from the deli to a full-service restaurant. I had never worked as a waitress before. I had a full time job and wanted to supplement my income with some part-time evenings at The Vineyards. To compensate for my inexperience, I concluded that working at an establishment with excellent food would keep the customers happy until I knew what I was doing! I learned quickly. Charles was an excellent teacher and an exacting taskmaster. He took pride in his food and wanted his staff to have the same pride in how his customers were served. I worked with a number of people who have become lifelong friends. We worked incredibly hard, but always managed to have a good time. The challenge of the steep stairs to the kitchen kept us all in great shape! I will always be grateful as well, for getting a chance to know the entire Pirtle family. Yes, Charles was my "boss" for quite a few years, but more than that, we became very good friends. I will always remember his gift for mimicry and his ability to make everyone laugh when the "pressure was on" during a busy evening. I will always treasure all the original cards he sent me, made from whatever he had handy, and always funny. I have kept them all and look through them when I am in need of a good laugh. My years at the Vineyards were a special time and I will always look back on that time with fondness. All in all I worked at the Vineyards for 6 or 7 years. Each year seemed to bring more people to Weston to experience the little house that served such incredible food and the church across the street that produced such wonderful local wine. It was interesting to occasionally deal with a difficult customer. By the end of their meal, they would be won over by the always good food and friendly atmosphere. I learned so much about fine food and wine. My affection for both continue to this day, as well as for the Pirtle family and their continuing achievements.

—Judy Turner Davis

Memories—Eric Wells

I first met Patricia and Elbert Pirtle in 1996 and the memory is very clear. Patricia was the first guest I assisted when I began my new job and she has been a blessing ever since. Over the years, I have grown very close to the Pirtles as we have shared many tragedies and many joys. I was fortunate enough to work side by side with Patricia and Elbert at the winery for several months in an effort to help out during the busy season and was truly amazed by the operation. They are so warm and sincere and their customers absolutely adore them. I feel blessed to have these wonderful people in my life and am a better person for it. They compliment one another perfectly.
Oh yeah, and the apple pie is delicious!

Eric Wells

Memories—Michelle Davis DeHaven

I realize as I am writing this that I am approximately the same age now that Charles was when I met him. By the time HE was in his thirties he was already an accomplished chef, world traveler and had experiences most people only dream of. I remember listening to Charles tell of his times in New York with wonder. As I had never even left the small town of Weston, I was a teenager who just knew the "big city" had to be more exciting and wondrous than our small town—why on earth would he prefer the smaller scale of Weston? Lucky for all of us, he was at his best right here in Weston, proudly offering our quiet corner of the world a little panache with his gourmet food and crazy sense of humor.

I guess I was pretty lucky that Charles didn't mind a kid hanging around his restaurant as much as I did. I got to spend time with Mom when I could and while she worked. I loved to watch Charles in the kitchen. He would sometimes just be quiet, losing himself in what he was preparing and other times he would explain what he was doing. Unfortunately for my family today, I didn't pay as much attention as I should have because I can't even come close to the skills I used to witness in that kitchen. My all time favorite dish of his was Pork Medallions.

There is no doubt that Charles was an extremely talented chef. But most of all Charles was just a good person. He had a knack for making me laugh when I just didn't think I could. I know my Mom had her hands full, being a single mom with a hormonal teenager who was at times very moody. I look back and remember it used to make me so "mad" that Charles would cheer me up when I just wanted to be difficult. He would just know that I might need a smile and would do any one of his imitations and I was laughing in no time.

I will share with you two of my favorite days spent with Charles. The first was the day I graduated from high school, when he hosted a graduation party for me at The Vineyards. The day was fabulous and I felt incredibly special to be the guest of honor. The other was my eighteenth birthday. Charles said it was important to do something special on that day so that you would always remember it. He always knew the coolest places to visit and took Mom and me to the city where we went to different landmarks and a couple of clubs with the best jazz. I'm not sure what the name of the place was we stopped last but we all sat and just listened to the most wonderful piano player. I am grateful for all of my memories of Charles. He was my friend and I miss his great big smile.

—Michelle Davis DeHaven

Memories from Kate and Jack Parsons

Charles just showed up at the back door. It was a frosty fall morning and we were well into the Sunday paper and a pot of coffee. We gave him FYI and a cup of Joe and gathered around the fireplace. Eventually, we got into one of our favorite discussions about religion. We read aloud from The Course in Miracles, and Charles once again displayed such spiritual insights. He could be so plugged in.

As morning turned into afternoon, I started to fix a roast and Charles took over. We went to the garden and cut the last of the chives, rosemary, thyme and oregano. Lots of herbs! Cups full! He added onions and a nearly full bottle of leftover red wine. As the meat simmered the afternoon away, we raked leaves and pulled the dead morning glories off the garage. After adding carrots and potatoes to the gently bubbling pot, we loaded up the fireplace and the C.D. player. We opened a new bottle of wine and talked about music, politics and more religion.

When dinner was served, I couldn't believe I was eating roast. It was so fragrant, tender and juicy. The flavor was out of this world! In my lifetime, I know I'll never have a better meal. He took an ordinary roast and made it extraordinary. He took an ordinary day and made it memorable. He had a gift in that way. He took a ramshackle house and added ambiance, style, candlelight, flowers, great music, art, great food and wine and lots of teasing and laughter. Added together, it wasn't just a nice meal—it was magic!

*Interior Design of the Vineyards Restaurant
by Kate Parsons—Locust Grove*

Memory—Cheryl Schimmel

I have so many fond memories of good time and great food at The Vineyards with Charles but I always recall a day when Judy, Lynn, Patricia (Charles' Mother) and I were having lunch and Charles came out with a wonderful jam cake with a white glazed topping and of course we had to have a slice. The cake was so wonderful and of course perfect in design. I began to eat mine and it bought back a precious memory of my Grandmother Hunt who made a jam cake, so I shared the memory with my group and Charles. I was ready to leave and Charles brought out the cake and said to take it home to share with my family because of the memory it triggered of my Grandmother. When I think of Charles it is always the first thought I have of his talents with food and warm generosity. I miss the charm Charles brought to Weston.

—Cheryl Schimmel

I met Charles, when he was just starting the restaurant, it was a small deli. We became friends and later I worked for him on Friday and Saturday nights. The pace was always fast and furious as we delivered wonderful food, with Charles coming up to see a special couple or group. Or he would occasionally show off a pie fresh from the oven. Later, whenever Charles traveled, he would send me postcards. Some were photographs converted to a postcard or odd pieces of something that he found. Some had glitter or stickers, some with cut outs, all unique, all Charles. Most arriving with just my first name, city and state. Sometimes a street name with or without a house number. Sometimes with a nickname he would call me. Luckily, we lived in Weston, as no other post office would probably have delivered those cards. But they were always sent from travels or where he was living at the time. He took me to the Netherlands in the spring when the flowers were in bloom. We both shared a love of gardening. I had a great friend in Charles. I saved all the gifts he gave me, rocks, shells, vases, paper weights, and lots of memories. I miss him still but I have the postcards.

—Jan Specht

The Beet Story

Charles gave Jesse and me a bunch of fresh beets from the garden he grew behind the restaurant . . . . I cooked them right away and served them for dinner. Shortly after Jesse and I had finished dinner and had enjoyed some of the beets. Charles just happened to drop in, I offered him some of the left-over beets so that he would know we had enjoyed them. He took a bite of the beets and finished up all that was left. A few weeks later he was in California; he called to get the beet recipe. This is how I cooked Charles' Beets. I cut all but 2 inches off the tops, left the beets whole and left the root end on; boiled in water until tender; drained and ran cold water over them; slipped off the skins and root ends. When they were cool, slice them. For about 16 ounces of sliced beets. Boil ½ cup vinegar, 1 cup sugar, 1/8 tsp. Ginger and 3 sticks of cinnamon in a sauce pan. After this has boiled, pour over beets. Chill several hours or overnight in refrigerator. Note: add a little vinegar to the water in which beets are boiled; this helps preserve the color of the beets . . . I have Many memories of Charles but this is my favorite . . . . With love Mary Pepper.

First Winery License

When I first applied for our winery license in the old church building, Jesse Pepper (Mary's husband) was mayor of Weston. I needed city council approval for the zoning and license. City hall at that time was at the corner of Main and Short street, where it had been since the beginning. Although I had been in business for two years in Weston at another location, I still felt like a rank outsider and was apprehensive. Jesse made me feel at home and the city council approved the zoning and license. It was an unforgettable experience.

Elbert Pirtle

www.ingramcontent.com/pod-product-compliance
Lightning Source LLC
Chambersburg PA
CBHW021114080526
44587CB00010B/513